THE
MISSISSIPPI
and West

by
LINDA THOMPSON

Rourke
Publishing LLC
Vero Beach, Florida 32964

www.rourkepublishing.com

PHOTO CREDITS:
Courtesy Bureau of Land Management: pages 18, 27, 31, 39; Courtesy of General Libraries, University of Texas at Austin: pages 12, 40; Courtesy Library of Congress, Prints and Photographs Division: pages 10, 14, 15, 16, 17, 19, 20-21, 22, 24, 29, 32, 34, 36, 37; Courtesy NASA: page 11; Courtesy National Parks Service: Title page, pages 7, 42; Courtesy National Archives and Records Administration: page 9; Courtesy Nebraska State Historical Society: Cover; Courtesy Northwestern University Library, Edward S. Curtis Collection: pages 8, 13, 22, 28, 38, 40; Courtesy Rohm Padilla: page 4.

SPECIAL NOTE: Further information about people's names shown in the text in bold can be found on page 43. More information about glossary terms in bold in the text can be found on pages 46 and 47.

DESIGN: ROHM PADILLA
LAYOUT/PRODUCTION: LUCY PADILLA

Library of Congress Cataloging-in-Publication Data

Thompson, Linda, 1941-
    The Mississippi and West / Linda Thompson.
        p. cm. --   (The expansion of America)
    Includes bibliographical references and index.
    ISBN 1-59515-224-5
    1.   United States--Territorial expansion--Juvenile literature. 2.   Frontier and pioneer life--United States--Juvenile literature.   I. Title. II. Series: Thompson, Linda, 1941-   Expansion of America.
    E179.5.T53 2004
    978'.02--dc22

                    2004010032

TITLE PAGE IMAGE
Native Americans transacting business in a frontier trading post

TABLE OF CONTENTS

Only 20 years after it became independent, the United States gained a region that doubled the country's size. And barely 50 years later, it reached across immense plains and towering mountain

OREGON TERRITORY 1846

ESTABLISHED 1818

CEDED BY MEXICO 1848

LOUISIANA PURCHASE 1803

GADSDEN PURCHASE 1853

TEXAS ANNEXED 1845

Map of major land additions to the continental United States ranges to touch the Pacific Ocean. How it grew so fast in such a short time is still an amazing tale.

One driving force to enlarge the country related to Americans' desires to control the main avenues of trade. One of the most important was the broad Mississippi River—but its **mouth**, or outlet to the sea, at New Orleans, had been in the hands of either the French or the Spanish since the 17th century.

In early 1803, the young United States was a weak country surrounded by three powerful foreign countries—Great Britain, France, and Spain. The United States consisted of only 17 states and one large **territory**, the "Northwest Territory," south and west of the Great Lakes. On the north, Great Britain controlled Canada and the Pacific Northwest. France owned Louisiana, while Spain had possession of Florida, Texas, and the entire Southwest, including California.

UNITED STATES PRIOR TO 1803

CEDED BY SPAIN 1819

People were urged to settle and farm in territory whose claim was in dispute.

Great Britain and France were historic **rivals** and had been fighting for years in Europe and other parts of the world. Because their wars were mainly about land, the United States feared being taken over by these powers if they brought their quarrels to America. In addition, people living in the less developed parts of the United States were more interested in their trading relationships than in whether they were **citizens** of one particular country or another. Residents of the southern states traded with the Spanish and French. Americans in the northern Mississippi Valley traded with the French and British. American politicians in the backwoods were urging groups of settlers to **secede** from the United States and join Spain or Canada or form an independent nation. President **George Washington** and others worried that the new country could be broken into pieces if the federal government failed to provide attractive conditions to settlers and traders.

In the early 1780s, Connecticut, Virginia, North and South Carolina, and Georgia claimed that their boundaries reached indefinitely westward because original charters from Great Britain had promised them "sea-to-sea" limits. But they could not defend their claims past the known **frontier**. To strengthen these claims, states encouraged farmers to settle in these undefined "Western Reserves." Land speculators also sold large tracts of land in the Western Reserves—which the **speculators** did not legally own—to people willing to settle there. So European Americans steadily moved into territory that the federal government had promised to Native Americans, pushing the Native groups further westward.

President George Washington

NATIVE RIGHTS

Since the 17th century, Native groups had been forced inland as coastal lands and river basins were settled. In spite of government attempts to protect their rights, most people saw Native Americans as obstacles and did not agree with the Native idea that the land is for the use of everyone.

Native Americans roamed freely across much of the country during the early 19th century.

By the end of 1803, President **Thomas Jefferson** had responded to a rare opportunity. He had purchased the vast and unknown Louisiana Territory from France, which included the vital port of New Orleans. "Louisiana" was the name of all of the land stretching from the Mississippi River to the Rocky Mountains. Nobody was certain about its southern and western boundaries at the time. But when the boundaries had been defined, it became clear that Jefferson had purchased 828,000 square miles (2,144,510 square km) of land. That land was now available for exploration and settlement.

Within half a century, the United States had also moved to gain Florida, Texas, the Southwest, California, and the Pacific Northwest. By 1853, the **continental** United States had taken on its current size and shape, not counting Alaska. The challenge of exploring all of this newly acquired territory

President Thomas Jefferson

was immense. But Americans were equal to the challenge. By 1869, a **transcontinental** railroad linked the 3,500 miles (5,633 km) or more of wilderness between the two coasts. The land suddenly became more accessible to explorers, settlers, and people bringing supplies and mail.

Book containing the documents of the Louisiana Purchase

9

Railroad through the Utah mountains, early 1900s

By 1900, the United States had six times as many people as in 1803, and 25 percent of them lived west of the Mississippi. Within a few **decades**, improvements such as roads, railroads, and the telegraph had made it much easier for those who settled the West to travel, to receive mail and supplies, and to live comfortably in their adopted homelands. These changes had huge impacts on the lives of the three million Native Americans who lived between the Mississippi River and the Pacific Ocean. Settling the wilderness led to the creation of cities and states and to the rise of industries—such as ranching, mining, and logging—that centered on the rich resources of the West.

Chapter II: LOUIS'S LAND

"Mississippi" is an **Algonquian** word that means "father of waters." The Mississippi River has always been an important transportation **artery** of North America. It is the second longest river, after the Missouri, in the United States, and drains surface water from all or part of 31 states into the Gulf of Mexico.

The delta of the Mississippi River as it flows into the Gulf of Mexico

Hernando de Soto

The first European to explore the Mississippi River was Hernando de Soto of Spain in 1541-1542. In the late 17th century, French explorers traveled down the river from the north. **René Robert Cavelier, Sieur de La Salle**, reached the mouth of the Mississippi in 1682 and claimed the whole valley for his king, **Louis XIV** of France, naming it "Louisiane," or "Louis's land."

Louisiana began at New Orleans and stretched northward, widening greatly, all the way to Canada. Its eastern border was the Mississippi River, and its western border skirted the Red River in Texas and then followed the spine of the Rocky Mountains. Out of Louisiana, eventually, came all of South Dakota, Nebraska, Iowa, Kansas, Missouri, Arkansas and Oklahoma, and most of Montana, Wyoming, and North Dakota. In addition, at least half of Louisiana, Colorado, and Minnesota, as well as pieces of New Mexico and Texas, were carved out of the land covered by the Louisiana Purchase.

Europeans lived on less than one percent of this land in 1800, although native Prairie groups had been living along river valleys such as the Missouri, the Platte, and the Ohio for centuries. About 40,000 people lived along the lower Mississippi. Most were **Creole** (French-American) settlers and their African-American slaves. Only a few military forts and trading posts had been built west of the Mississippi. Most of the rest of Louisiana was the home of **nomadic** Plains groups of Native Americans, who roamed huge areas of land pursuing **migrating** buffalo herds.

The west was once a vast wilderness with thousands of roaming buffalo.

THE UNIQUE MAKEUP OF NEW ORLEANS

Great Britain, France, and Spain were the main **colonizers** of less developed countries, including the islands of the **West Indies**. The closeness of these islands to New Orleans influenced the social and cultural makeup of the lower Mississippi Valley. Native Americans, French, Spanish, Anglo-American, and African people who had been brought from the West Indies to New Orleans as slaves mixed together in a society that was quite different from any other in America.

Members of an evangelic group from Louisiana with Sioux from South Dakota, including Chief Spotted Crow

In 1787, Congress had passed the Northwest Ordinance, setting forth the laws by which new states would develop. As soon as a "district" had a population of 5,000 males (not including slaves), it could elect a territorial government. With 60,000 people, it could become a state. An important provision of this act stated "There shall be neither slavery nor **involuntary servitude** in said territory."

In 1800, Thomas Jefferson was elected president of the United States. Jefferson sent **James Monroe** to France in March 1803 to attempt to buy New Orleans from **Napoleon Bonaparte**, emperor of France. With the help of the United States minister there, **Robert Livingston**,

Coin celebrating the statehood of Louisiana

the United States was able to buy all of Louisiana for $15 million. The treaty gave Louisiana residents all the rights of American citizens, including the ability to form states according to the Northwest Ordinance.

The Northwest Ordinance stated that a developing territory could not have slavery, leading many former slaves to move northward.

This purchase turned out to be the best bargain in American history, but at the time, it was full of potential problems. For one thing, a strict interpretation of the Constitution suggested that the president did not have the right to increase the size of the country or to promise people outside United States boundaries that they could become citizens. But Jefferson sent the treaty to Congress before Napoleon could change his mind. The Senate **ratified** the treaty, and Louisiana became United States territory.

The Louisiana Purchase secured the Mississippi River and its mouth for trade and exploration, but at the time many Americans believed that it was not a smart move. People feared that settlers in the huge land of Louisiana would be so scattered that they would be ungovernable. The boundaries, especially near Spanish-controlled Texas and New Mexico, were not clear. Native peoples inhabiting the region were unknown and therefore feared.

Napoleon Bonaparte

Jefferson argued that feeding a rapidly growing country such as the United States required large agricultural areas. Without such areas, the country might follow the European pattern of becoming overpopulated, leading to inequality between the classes and warfare. He proposed that the United States would be an "empire of liberty," rather than the old kind of empire, which involved a "mother" country selling the resources of her colonies.

TO GROW OR NOT?

Aaron Burr

American leaders disagreed about how fast the country should grow. After the Louisiana Purchase, **Aaron Burr**, who was vice president under Jefferson, led a **conspiracy** to separate New England and New York from the United States. Some New York politicians joined Burr in this plan, but **Alexander Hamilton** discovered the plot and it failed. Burr challenged Hamilton to a duel and killed him. Then Burr conspired with **James Wilkinson**, governor of the new Louisiana Territory, to conquer Mexico and form a country out of Louisiana and Mexico. But Wilkinson betrayed Burr, who was arrested and tried for **treason**. He was **acquitted** on the grounds that he had not performed treason, only plotted it.

Chapter III: EXPLORERS, TRAPPERS, AND MOUNTAIN MEN

President Jefferson had been planning to send an expedition to explore the Pacific Northwest, which was claimed by both the United States and Britain. Before making the Louisiana Purchase, he had already discussed such an expedition with his personal secretary, **Meriwether Lewis**. He immediately asked Lewis to put the trip together.

Like many people of the time, President Jefferson believed that a river must run westward from the Missouri to the Pacific Ocean. This "Northwest Passage" turned out not to exist, as Lewis and **William Clark** found during their famous exploration in 1804-1806. About 45 men—young explorers, soldiers, and French river guides—joined them as they set out from St. Louis, Missouri, in 1804.

The joining place of the Missouri and Marias rivers, in Montana, was named Decision Point by Lewis and Clark.

Meriwether Lewis · William Clark

This "**Corps** of Discovery" traveled more than 8,000 miles (12,870 km) in two years, four months, and ten days. They spent the winter of 1805-1806 near the mouth of the Columbia River on the Oregon coast. Upon their return, they reported to President Jefferson, and then sat down to prepare their journals for publication, a task that took eight years. One of their men, Sergeant **Patrick Gass**, published his journal sooner, and it inspired other American frontiersmen to head up the Missouri to explore the northern part of the Louisiana Purchase.

General Zebulon Pike

In 1806, the United States government also sent **Zebulon Pike** to explore the southern part of the new territory. Pike left St. Louis, Missouri, with 22 men in two barges. At what is now the Missouri-Kansas border, they exchanged their barges for horses and traveled into present-day Colorado. There, they tried to climb a mountain in the **Front Range**, but failed. Later, the peak was named Pikes Peak. The explorers ended up inside Spanish territory and were arrested and taken to Santa Fe. They were released some months later. Although the Spanish had taken Pike's maps and notebooks, his good memory allowed him to report back to President Jefferson on what he had seen.

The summit of Pikes Peak, named after the general and explorer

The southern portion of the Louisiana Purchase, the land just west and north of New Orleans, became attractive to settlers right away. By 1809, 14,000 new settlers had arrived, many of them from the West

Five generations of a family living on a plantation, 1862

Indies. In 1812, the state of Louisiana entered the union. Its population consisted mostly of planters and merchants, along with their African slaves.

But the less familiar parts of the Louisiana Purchase were settled more slowly. Congress had turned down President Jefferson's request to further explore the Mississippi and Missouri rivers and their **tributaries**. Little was done with the findings from the two early expeditions. It was up to **mountain men** and a few hardy pioneers to investigate the upper Missouri country, the Great Plains, and the Far West.

Navajo man and cowboy seated on a blanket playing cards

Beaver and other fur animals were once plentiful in the part of the Louisiana Purchase that is now Iowa, Minnesota, and North and South Dakota. But British and French-Canadian traders, assisted by Native Americans who trapped for them, had been well established in the region for many years. The border between the United States and Canada had never been well defined, so British traders regularly invaded the Great Lakes region and streams to the west.

Muskrat skins hanging to dry beside a Spanish trapper's home. They will then be taken to Louisiana and sold.

To strengthen American fur trading rights in these northern parts, William Clark and others formed the Missouri Fur Company. In 1809, they began building trading posts such as **Fort Mandan** in what is now North Dakota. These trappers and traders had a difficult time establishing themselves because of frequent attacks by Native groups such as the **Piegan** people in Montana. Also, British companies, especially the **North West Company**, did everything they could to block the American fur trade.

Great Britain, Spain, Russia, and the United States had all claimed "Oregon Country." It included the present states of Idaho, Washington, and Oregon, as well as much of British Columbia, Canada. Britain's **Hudson's Bay Company**, one of the oldest fur-trading businesses, had a firm foothold in this region, and its headquarters was at Fort Vancouver on the Columbia River. But a German **immigrant**, **John Jacob Astor**, founded the **Pacific Fur Company** in 1808 and sent an expedition by sea to the mouth of the Columbia River, where they built **Astoria**. Here, the American fur-trading industry had a promising start. But as the **War of 1812** got underway, Astor learned that a British warship was approaching. Unable to defend Astoria, he sold the structure and his business to the North West Company.

A pioneer man and son

Fur traders setting out from Independence (near present-day Kansas City, Missouri) blazed trails that later grew into famous pioneer wagon trail routes, such as the Santa Fe, Oregon, and California trails. The traders became acquainted with various Native American groups, and through that contact began to change their lives. They weakened tribes by turning them against each other and also by selling alcohol and spreading disease. But some of the mountain men's actions were less destructive. Many married Native women and had families. Some mountain men joined Native tribes and even became chiefs.

JAMES BECKWOURTH

James P. Beckwourth was a typical mountain man. Son of a white father and an African-American slave, he joined one of Ashley's expeditions as a blacksmith. He became comfortable living in the wilderness, married a Crow woman, and joined the Crow tribe. His skills at hunting, trapping, and mountain living made him a valuable addition, and eventually he was made a Crow chief.

RENDEZVOUS SYSTEM

In 1825, a Missouri trader, **William Henry Ashley**, invented the "rendezvous system." It allowed mountain men to stay in the Rocky Mountains and not have to travel back to Missouri for supplies. He instructed his trappers to spread out seeking beaver and then meet, at a given date, at Henry's Fork on the Green River to exchange their furs for supplies. For years afterward, most trappers lived in the mountains, gathering at a **rendezvous** point in the spring. The rendezvous resembled a Native trade fair and provided a badly needed social function. Trappers, settlers, Mexican traders, and thousands of Indians traded, gambled, and celebrated for weeks until it was time to begin trapping again.

The Green River, Utah, was one of the first rendezvous points for trading.

Chapter IV: **WAGON TRAINS AND GOLDEN VEINS**

The arch in St. Louis is a symbol of the city's role in westward expansion.

After the War of 1812, westward **migration** increased. Missouri Territory (the future state of Missouri) began to attract farmers, as the threat of Native American attack had lessened. By 1817, more than 60,000 people had settled in St. Louis and westward along the Missouri River. Missouri became a state in 1821, and by 1830 its eastern half was well populated. Arkansas followed with statehood in 1836 and Iowa 10 years later.

The **pioneers** who followed the trappers and traders into the West came mainly from the Mississippi Valley. These people were used to frontier life and the hardships that came with it. Many of them had migrated to the Mississippi Valley when it was the frontier. Between 1825 and 1845, these hardy families moved into Spanish Texas, New Mexico, and California, not troubled by the uncertainties of living under a foreign power. Beginning in 1841, they began to move into Oregon Country, first by the hundreds and later by the thousands.

The earth is still scarred from wagon wheels of travelers who moved west on America's trails.

Meanwhile, Native groups had been pushed from their homelands east of the Mississippi onto unwanted vacant land west of the 95th **meridian**. This was the western edge of Arkansas. The unwanted land first became "Indian Territory," and in 1907 it became part of the state of Oklahoma.

An elder of the Cheyenne

HOW INDIANS LOST OUT

From the beginning, the United States recognized Indian tribes as **sovereign**. They were considered nations within a larger nation, and only the federal government could negotiate with them and buy their land. But in practice, this policy was ignored. While upholding sovereignty, the U.S. Supreme Court ruled that Indian nations were **wards** of the federal government. This interpretation implied that Natives were weak and dependent, like children. It allowed individual states and the U.S. Congress to **relocate** Native tribes when European Americans wanted their land.

From about 1800, a few American traders and farmers had begun moving from the lower Mississippi Valley westward into Texas, which was part of Spain's empire. The Spanish discouraged these foreign intruders, sometimes with armed attacks. But after Mexico became independent from Spain in 1821, the Mexican state of Texas began to welcome immigrants. Residents of the Lower Mississippi Valley, who continually fought **malaria** and **dysentery** caused by dampness and mosquitoes, were eager to move to the dryer, more healthful climate of Texas.

Soldiers from Mexico became tolerant of pioneers after Mexico gained its independence.

By 1830, nearly 8,000 Americans had moved to Texas, with an additional 1,000 slaves. There were only about 3,500 Mexicans in Texas, and cultural differences led to rebellious feelings among the Americans. The Mexican government sent an Army to San Antonio to prevent any rebellion, and in February 1836, 187 Americans met 6,000 Mexican troops in a fierce battle at the **Alamo** Mission. All of the Americans (including frontiersmen Davy Crockett and Jim Bowie) died, but they first managed to kill 1,544 Mexican soldiers. A month later, the Americans in Texas declared independence, rallying around the cry, "Remember the Alamo!" In April 1836, the Americans defeated the Mexican troops in the **Battle of San Jacinto**. Texas became an independent **republic**, although Mexico did not officially recognize it as such.

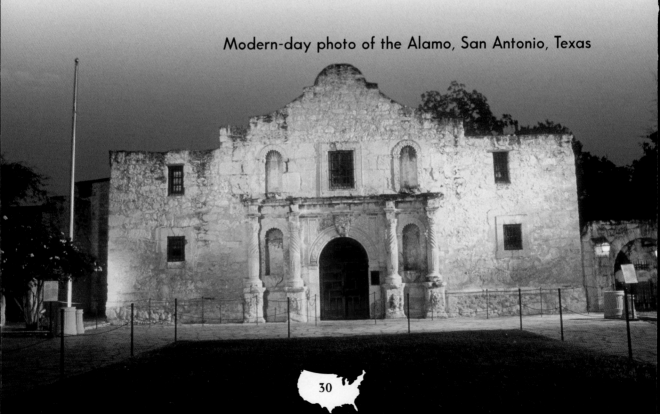

Modern-day photo of the Alamo, San Antonio, Texas

A man dressed as a pioneer

Beginning in 1821, traders took **caravans** to Santa Fe, New Mexico, which was first ruled by Spain and then by Mexico. Some traders, such as **William Becknell**, remained in Santa Fe and founded businesses there. Others followed the "**Old Spanish Trail**" from Santa Fe to present-day Los Angeles, California. Some of them preferred California's mild climate and fertile soil, obtained Mexican land grants, and remained as ranchers.

By 1865, 250,000 people had traveled west with one basic rule—follow the rivers. They left their schools, churches, stores, and doctors behind them, and also the rule of law. They would either have to carry their food or find it along the way. Independence, Missouri, was their "jumping-off point."

A Mormon wagon train headed west

From 1840, small caravans took the **Oregon Trail** from Independence, and by 1843, large wagon trains were carrying settlers across the Rocky Mountains into Oregon's Willamette Valley or to northern California's foothills. In 1847, several hundred **Mormons** migrated from Illinois to the Great Salt Lake, Utah. Thousands of other Mormons followed them, built Salt Lake City, and, using skillful **irrigation** methods, turned the rocky desert into fertile farmland.

View of Salt Lake City, Utah, late 1800s

As large masses of people moved into foreign lands such as Oregon or California, they pressured the federal government to make their new homelands part of the United States. For example, American settlers in the Willamette Valley let President **James K. Polk** know that they wanted the uncertainty about the country's northern boundary settled. Polk had been elected in 1844 on an **expansionist platform**. He wanted both Texas and Oregon to become part of the United States, but he claimed that "Oregon" extended northward as far as the 54° 40' **latitude**. This is well into what is now northern Canada. In 1845, Great Britain offered the 49th parallel as the border. On June 10, 1846, the 49th **parallel** became the boundary between the United States and British Territory.

The Texans had asked the United States for statehood several times, but slavery in Texas was an issue. Finally, in December 1845, the United States Congress passed a resolution to **annex** Texas. It passed over the objections of those who opposed slavery, and Texas became a state.

President Polk was also determined to acquire California by peaceful means if possible. After several attempts at negotiating a purchase failed, the **Mexican War** began. As a result, in 1848 the United States annexed California, New Mexico, and the entire Southwest, gaining 529,000 square miles (1,370,000 km) of land.

The single most important factor in bringing people to the Far West was the California Gold Rush, which began in 1849. By 1860, 380,000 people lived in the new state of California. Some settlers never reached California, running out of money and remaining in Kansas, Colorado, or Nevada instead. Others failed to make a strike and moved somewhere else. Later discoveries of silver and gold in Nevada and Colorado attracted some of these pioneer families. Between 1858 and 1875, miners wandered all over the West searching for the yellow glint of gold in streams and mountainsides. Only a few hit "pay dirt," but when they did the news brought thousands of people to the area. They formed towns, such as Virginia City, Nevada, which turned into ghost towns when the vein of metal ore ran out.

Gold and rumors of gold brought even more explorers and miners.

A Concord Coach

Between 1850 and 1870, settlers and miners pressured the government to improve communication and transportation between the far-flung settlements. Mail took 30 days to reach California from the East by ship, and cost 12 to 80 cents an ounce (per 31 grams). In 1857, a company belonging to **John Butterfield** and **William G. Fargo** of New York was selected to open a stagecoach line from Tipton, Missouri, to San Francisco. The Overland Mail Company introduced "Concord Coaches" to carry passengers and mail.

These coaches had heavy iron wheels and an iron-reinforced body, and were pulled by four horses or six mules. They could carry nine people and had a triangular "boot" in the rear for luggage and mail sacks. On September 15, 1858, one coach set out from Tipton and another from San Francisco. They raced each other to their destinations and on October 10, 24 days after leaving Tipton, the westbound coach arrived in San Francisco. But the eastbound coach had beaten it, taking only 21 days to reach Missouri. Freight companies also formed, using oxen-drawn wagons to carry supplies to Army camps and mining fields.

Homesteaders outside their log cabin

In the 1850s, the United States Interior Department set up the Pacific Wagon Road Office to build roads needed by the new settlers. Helped by soldiers from the Corps of Topographical Engineers, they built 34 roads in the West from 1850 to 1860. These roads greatly reduced the stress of frontier travel and were an important first step in developing the region. Also in the 1850s, small railroads had been built, such as the Missouri Pacific Railroad, which connected St. Louis and Kansas City, Missouri. The country's leaders began to discuss the idea of a railroad that reached from East Coast to West Coast, and in 1853 Congress authorized a survey of all possible routes between the Mississippi Valley and the Pacific Ocean. It took only 16 more years to make the dream of a transcontinental railroad a reality.

In 1862, Congress passed the **Homestead Act** to encourage young people and immigrants to start new lives as independent landowners. The Act granted 160 acres (65 hectares) to anyone who would live on the land and farm it. If a settler wished to buy the land after living there six months, the cost was only $1.25 an acre (.41 hectare).

PONY EXPRESS

From April 1860 to October 1861, the Pony Express carried mail with remarkable speed. The Central Overland California and Pikes Peak Express Company built 190 stations between San Francisco, California, and St. Joseph, Missouri, a distance of nearly 2,000 miles (3,218 km). The company chose 500 horses for speed and endurance and advertised in the California newspapers. Riders were paid $100 a month. Horses traveled an average of 10 miles (16 km) per hour. The fastest mail delivery was of President **Abraham Lincoln's Inaugural** Address to the West Coast in 7 days and 17 hours. But the Pony Express ended in a short time because of financial loss and the outbreak of the Civil War.

A man from the Pony Express riding through Indian territory

Native Americans still lived freely in the Great Basin and the Plains until the **Civil War** (1861-1865). More than 150,000 Great Basin people lived in eastern California alone. Gradually, miners and settlers drove them out, leaving only a few hundred survivors to be placed on reservations by 1890. The Ute in Utah were forced onto **reservations** by 1861. But Southwest groups such as the **Apache** and **Navajo** fought harder. The United States placed 1,500 Army troops along the trails in military forts to subdue them.

Navajo people in the desert

KIT CARSON AND THE NAVAJO

Apache and Navajo people fought desperately to remain in their lands but in 1863-64, Colonel **Kit Carson** led Army troops in killing 664 Natives and capturing 8,793. Carson and his troops drove 6,000 Navajo from their homeland to **Fort Sumner** in eastern New Mexico. The Apache were also rounded up and moved to reservations, but many warriors escaped and raided travelers and settlers for another decade. When many Navajo died at Fort Sumner, the government finally allowed the rest of the tribe to return to the northern New Mexico-Arizona region, where they live today.

The Plains people were the most difficult to control. The **Sioux**, **Cheyenne**, **Kiowa**, and **Comanche** were skilled horsemen and fierce warriors. In 1859, a large number of miners crossed the Plains, which set off persistent conflict. Indian agents tricked or bribed some chiefs into renouncing claims to their lands, but large numbers of Natives rebelled and refused to surrender. In 1864, Cheyenne and **Arapaho** groups went on the **warpath**. From the North Platte River to the Arkansas River, they murdered settlers, burned homes, destroyed mail stations, and left a path of ruin. The Army retaliated with a massacre of unarmed Native families at Sand Creek (in what is now southern Colorado). Subsequent wars took their toll on Native populations until the **Battle of Wounded Knee** in 1890 spelled an end to Native resistance. By 1883, the buffalo had been nearly **exterminated** as well. (By 1903, only 34 free roaming buffalo were left in the United States.)

Almost all the buffalo had been killed by the early 1900s.

President
Grover
Cleveland

In 1887, President **Grover Cleveland** signed the **Dawes Act**, allowing tribal lands to be divided. Native families were given 160 acres (65 hectares) each, and the remaining land was sold to non-Natives. By 1890, about two million people had taken advantage of the Dawes and Homestead acts. They had built some 372,660 farms in the West. But these farms were only successful in states with plenty of water. In other very dry parts of the country, a 160-acre (65-hectare) farm was not large enough or fertile enough to support a family.

A party of Oglala Sioux on a hill overlooking the valley of Wounded Knee Creek, Pine Ridge reservation, in South Dakota

Railroads gave a major economic boost to the fledgling country.

At this point a unique American industry, which began in southern Texas in the early 19th century—cattle ranching—began to spread over the West. Two decades after the Civil War, herds of longhorn cattle guarded by cowboys on horseback could be seen throughout the Great Plains. Soon, new, meatier breeds of cattle were developed. In just six states—Kansas, Nebraska, Wyoming, Montana, North Dakota, and South Dakota—the numbers of cattle went from 130,650 in 1860 to 4,418,000 in 1880. The development of railroads gave the cattle industry an important boost, as trains of cattle cars replaced the 1,000-mile (1,600-km) cattle drives from western states to the stockyards in cities such as Chicago.

New Mexico and Arizona, the 47th and 48th states, were admitted to the union in 1912. In the 100 years following 1880, the population of the United States nearly **quintupled**. Part of this increase came from the 40 million immigrants who arrived from countries all over the world. Today, 38 percent of American people, including most Native Americans, live in the West.

A desire to preserve what was left of the beauty and wildness of the West led to the establishment of the **National Park Service** (1916). Yellowstone National Park, the oldest of the national parks, was named in 1872. Many of the pioneering trails have been designated **National Historic Trails**, including those taken to Oregon, California, and Santa Fe. The Lewis and Clark Trail, Mormon Pioneer Trail, and Pony Express Trail are also National Historic Trails. Students of American history can travel these trails and recreate the experience of the 19th century people who explored and populated the West.

Horse-drawn carriage in front of the Roosevelt Arch in Yellowstone National Park, 1912

Ashley, William Henry (1778-1838) - American fur-trader and politician; United States Congressman, 1831-1837.

Astor, John Jacob (1763-1848) - United States merchant and fur-trader born in Germany; became one of the wealthiest men in America.

Becknell, William (1796?-1865) - U.S. trader and explorer known as the "Father of the Santa Fe Trail."

Beckwourth, James P. (1798-1866) - Blacksmith and mountain man who became a member of the Crow tribe.

Bonaparte, Napoleon (1769-1821)- French Army officer who seized power after the French Revolution, and in 1804 named himself emperor.

Burr, Aaron (1756-1836) - Vice president of the United States who was tried for treason in 1807.

Butterfield, John (1801-1869) - Owner of the Overland Mail Company and co-founder of American Express.

Carson, Kit (1809-1868) - U.S. trapper, guide, and soldier; Indian agent for the Ute and Apache at Taos, New Mexico; eventually took command of Fort Garland in western Colorado.

Clark, William (1770-1838) - U.S. Army officer who, along with Meriwether Lewis, led the exploration of the Louisiana Purchase (1804-1806).

Cleveland, Grover (1837-1908) - The 22nd and 24th president of the United States.

Fargo, William G. (1818-1881) - Co-founder of the Overland Mail Company and co-founder and president of Wells, Fargo & Co. from 1870 to 1872.

Gass, Patrick (1771-1870) - A member of the Corps of Discovery who was first to publish his journal of the expedition.

Hamilton, Alexander (1755-1804) - First secretary of the treasury under George Washington.

Jefferson, Thomas (1743-1826) - Third president of the U.S. (1801-1809).

La Salle, René Robert Cavelier, Sieur de (1643-1687) - French explorer, first European to travel the length of the Mississippi River.

Lewis, Meriwether (1774-1809) - Secretary to President Jefferson and U.S. explorer who led, with William Clark, the first exploration of the Louisiana Purchase (1804-1806).

Lincoln, Abraham (1809-1865) - The 16th president of the United States (1861-1865).

Livingston, Robert (1746-1813) - U.S. diplomat who helped negotiate the Louisiana Purchase.

Louis XIV (1638-1715) - King of France (1643-1715), known as the "Sun King."

Monroe, James (1758-1831) - Fifth president of the U.S. (1817-1825).

Pike, Zebulon (1779-1813) - U.S. explorer in the Louisiana Territory, Colorado, and New Mexico. Pikes Peak in Colorado was named after him.

Polk, James K. (1795-1849) - 11th president of the U.S. (1845-1849).

Washington, George (1732-1799) - First president of the United States (1789-1797).

Wilkinson, James (1757-1825) - U.S. general who took part in several conspiracies to divide the country and was Louisiana's governor from 1805 to 1806.

A Timeline of the History of
— The Mississippi and West —

1541-1542   Spanish explorer Hernando de Soto explores the Mississippi River.

1682   French explorer René Robert Cavelier, Sieur de La Salle explores the Mississippi River Valley, claims it for King Louis XIV of France, and names Louisiana after him.

1775-1783   The American Revolution ends with the 13 former British colonies forming a new country, the United States of America.

1787   Congress passes the Northwest Ordinance.

1803   President Jefferson buys Louisiana Territory for $15 million.

1804-1806   Lewis and Clark explore the northern and northwestern sections of the Louisiana Purchase.

1806   Zebulon Pike explores the southern section of the Louisiana Purchase.

1811   John Jacob Astor builds Astoria, the first American outpost on the West Coast.

1807-1814   Journals from the Lewis and Clark Expedition are published.

1812-1815   The War of 1812.

1819   Florida is acquired from Spain.

1820-1830   American settlers move to Texas, a Mexican state.

1821   Opening of the Santa Fe Trail.

1836	The Battle of the Alamo and the Battle of San Jacinto lead to independence for Texas.
1843	The first major wagon train carries more than 1,000 settlers along the Oregon Trail to Oregon.
1844	James Polk is elected president on an expansionist platform.
1845	The United States annexes Texas.
1846	The U.S. border with British territory is established at the 49th parallel.
1846-1848	The Mexican War adds California and the Southwest to the United States.
1847-48	Mormon pioneers settle Salt Lake City, Utah.
1849	The California Gold Rush begins. By 1860, California's population has soared to 380,000.
1857	Opening of the first overland mail and stagecoach route.
1858-1875	Miners strike gold and other minerals all over the West, forming new towns that become ghost towns after a few years.
1860-1861	The Pony Express takes mail from St. Joseph, Missouri, to San Francisco.
1862	Congress passes the Homestead Act, and by 1890 two million people have moved into the West and claimed land.
1862-1869	Construction of a transcontinental railroad authorized by Congress and completed.
1887	The Dawes Act allows Native lands to be divided and sold.

GLOSSARY

acquit - To release completely from an obligation or accusation.

Alamo - Spanish mission in San Antonio, Texas, where the war for Texan independence from Mexico began.

Algonquian - Language of related groups of Native people who were widely distributed around North America.

annex - To add to something earlier, larger, or more important; to attach.

Apache - A group of Native Americans of the Southwest, who originally migrated from Canada.

Arapaho - A group of Native Americans of the Great Plains, ranging from Canada to Texas.

artery - A vessel that carries blood from the heart; a major channel or route of transportation.

Astoria - Port city in northwest Oregon, founded in 1811 by John J. Astor, the first permanent United States settlement on the west coast.

Battle of San Jacinto - A conflict in 1836 on the San Jacinto River, Texas, in which troops led by Sam Houston defeated 1,200 Mexicans and captured their general.

Battle of Wounded Knee - Final engagement in 1890 between Native Americans and European Americans, in which the 7th Cavalry killed more than 200 Sioux.

caravan - A company of travelers on a journey, especially in desert terrain.

Cheyenne - Group of Algonquian-speaking Native Americans who migrated from the Minnesota area onto the Great Plains in the 17th century.

citizen - A member of a state; a native or naturalized person who is faithful to a government and expects protection from it.

Civil War - War between factions inside a country; the American Civil War (1861-1865) over the right to own slaves.

colonizer - One who establishes a colony or settles a new land or region.

Comanche - A group of Native American nomadic people who ranged from Wyoming and Nebraska south into Texas and New Mexico, and who speak a Uto-Aztecan language.

conspiracy - The act of plotting together; a group of people who plot against an established government, program, or institution.

continental - Relating to a continent, especially the part of a country on a specific continent or land mass.

corps - A body of persons with a common activity or occupation.

Creole - A person descended from early French or Spanish settlers, or an American of mixed French or Spanish and African-American blood who speaks a dialect of French or Spanish.

Dawes Act - Law passed in 1887, named for Senator Henry L. Dawes, which ended the United States reservation system and forced the sale of Native lands.

decade - A period of 10 years.

dysentery - A disease marked by diarrhea and usually caused by infection.

expansionist - A person who believes that a nation should expand its territory.

exterminate - To get rid of completely by killing off.

Fort Mandan - A trading post that the Missouri Fur Company built as its headquarters in present-day North Dakota.

Fort Sumner - Army fort on the Pecos River in New Mexico, where Navajos were confined in the 1860s.

Front Range - Southern Rocky Mountains in Colorado and New Mexico.

frontier - A border between two countries; a region that is on the margin of developed territory.

Homestead Act - United States law of 1862 that encouraged westward expansion.

Hudson's Bay Company - Trading company founded in 1670 in England to promote fur trade in North America.

immigrant - A person who moves into a country from somewhere else.

inaugural - Marking a beginning; in the United States the newly elected president is inaugurated and gives an Inaugural Address to the nation.

involuntary servitude - In the position of working for someone else without choice.

irrigation - Watering land by artificial means.

Kiowa - A Native American people from the present-day states of Colorado, Kansas, New Mexico, Oklahoma, and Texas, who speak a common language.

latitude - An angular distance measured from the equator to scientifically describe a location on the Earth. Latitude lines run east-west and longitude lines run north-south.

malaria - A human disease caused by parasites in the red blood cells and spread by the bites of mosquitoes.

meridian - An imagined great circle on the surface of the Earth, passing through the poles, which marks longitude.

Mexican War - Conflict between Mexico and the United States in 1846-1848.

migrate - To move from one country or place to another.

migration - Movement from one country or place to another.

Mormon - Relating to the Church of Jesus Christ of Latter-day Saints.

mountain man - An American frontiersman who usually began as a beaver trapper and ended up as an explorer, guide, or settler.

mouth - An opening; the place where a stream enters a larger body of water.

National Historic Trail - A trail preserved by the 1968 National Trails System Act, which follows as closely as possible an original trail or route of national historic significance.

National Park System - A system of national parks, monuments, historic sites, and recreation areas founded in 1916 and managed by the National Park Service.

Navajo - Largest Native American group in the United States, speaking an Athabascan language and concentrated in the Southwest.

nomadic - Roaming about from place to place, without a fixed home.

North West Company - Canadian fur-trading company founded in the 1770s.

Old Spanish Trail - Trail founded between 1776 and 1820, originally to supply Spanish missions in California from Santa Fe, New Mexico.

Oregon Trail - Emigrant route to the Northwest, reaching from Independence, Missouri, to the mouth of the Columbia River.

Pacific Fur Company - A branch of the American Fur Company founded by John Jacob Astor.

parallel - When referring to latitude, a line running east-west around the globe and measured from the equator to describe a location on the Earth.

Piegan - A branch of the Blackfeet tribe of Native Americans in Montana.

pioneer - First in anything; one of the first to settle a territory.

platform - Declaration of principles and policies by a group or candidate.

quintuple - To make five times as great or as many.

ratify - To formally approve.

relocate - To move, establish, or lay out in a new place.

rendezvous - French for "present yourselves"; a place set for meeting.

republic - A government having a chief of state who is not a monarch, but usually a president.

reservation - A tract of public land set aside, as for Native Americans to live.

rival - A competitor or opponent.

secede - To withdraw from an organization or nation.

Sioux - Large Native American group that now lives mostly in the Dakotas and eastern Montana.

sovereign - Having supreme power.

speculator - A person who buys and sells expecting to profit from price changes.

territory - A geographical area; in the United States, an area under its control, with a separate legislature, but not yet a state.

transcontinental - Extending across a continent, such as a railway.

treason - The betrayal of a trust; attempt to overthrow a government.

tributary - A stream that feeds a larger stream or a lake.

War of 1812 - Conflict between the United States and Great Britain (1812-1815).

ward - A person who is under the guard or protection of a court or guardian.

warpath - The route taken by a party of people intent on making war.

West Indies - A large group of islands between the United States and South America, divided into the Bahamas, the Greater Antilles, and the Lesser Antilles.

INDEX

Books of Interest

Bernstein, Vivian. *America's History: Land of Liberty/Book 2*, Steck-Vaughn Company, 1997.

Blumberg, Rhoda. *What's the Deal? Jefferson, Napoleon and the Louisiana Purchase*, National Geographic Society, 1998.

Bruchac, Joseph. *Lasting Echoes: An Oral History of Native American People*, Harcourt, 1997. Paperback: Harper Trophy, 1999.

Burgan, Michael. *The Louisiana Purchase, We the People Series*, Compass Point Books, 2002.

Schanzer, Rosalyn. *How We Crossed the West: The Adventures of Lewis and Clark*, National Geographic, 2002.

Worth, Richard. *Westward Expansion and Manifest Destiny in American History*, Enslow Publishers, Inc., 2001.

Web Sites of Interest

http://americanwest.com/

http://www.earlyamerica.com

http://louisianapurchase.umsl.edu/

http://www.lapurchase.org/history.html

http://www.nationalgeographic.com/lewisand-clark/

http://www.usgennet.org/usa/topic/preservation/history/louis/toc.htm

Linda Thompson is a Montana native and a graduate of the University of Washington. She was a teacher, writer, and editor in the San Francisco Bay Area for 30 years and now lives in Taos, New Mexico. She can be contacted through her web site,

http://www.highmesaproductions.com